American Bird Watching for Beginners

By Johnny Pale

The Ultimate Guide to Bird Watching, Bird Identification, and the Top Bird Species in America

2nd Edition

Table of Contents

Introduction

I want to thank you and congratulate you for purchasing the book, *"American Bird Watching for Beginners: The Ultimate Guide to Bird Watching, Bird Identification, and the Top Bird Species in America"*.

This book contains proven steps and strategies on how to be a good birder and be able to identify different bird species especially the most popular ones.

Bird-watching is not only an eco-friendly hobby but it is also definitely enjoyable. It is addicting and educational. Bird-watching is not only for professionals and ornithologists; it is also recommended for all people who love nature. As easy as it may seem, bird-watching has certain requirements such as skills, patience, strategy, and basic knowledge on birds and their behavior. There are certain tools necessary to make this activity more fun and more fulfilling. These things are listed with the basic uses described in the book.

America is known for numerous bird species that you may observe even in just your backyard and this book will help to guide you on how to identify the different kinds of birds that thrive in America. So, if you want to become a certified birder, this book will assist you in making it happen in no time.

Thanks again for purchasing this book, I hope you enjoy it!

Chapter 1: Introduction to Bird Watching

Birds can be very interesting to watch. Each species is different from one another and these all exhibit varying physical characteristics and behaviors. According to experts, there are at least 970 species of birds found in the United States and Canada alone. That is just about a fraction in the total of about 10,000 bird species in the world. If you are aiming to be a good birder, your backyard may only give you at least 30 species (that is if you are really fortunate), but some locations may yield sightings of more than that number.

Bird watching entails more than just seeing birds. Seeing is different from watching because if you watch, you have to focus on the bird and you should be able to identify them or their species and observe. Bird identification is the most crucial part of being a birder or a birdwatcher. It is the final goal of bird watching. It requires patience, time, strategy, specific tools, and some basic knowledge and of, course one, needs to be totally interested.

For beginners, their own backyards should be their starting point. It is the best place to start observing bird behavior and physical attributes. They can also start learning the proper ways of feeding the birds and bringing them close enough so they can be observed properly. But it should not be too close to make them used to human presence. Bird watchers should be more aware of the environment than most. That is the reason why they observe the birds in their natural habitat with the last amount of human influence as much as possible.

One way to start is by placing bird baths where you can easily spot them. Bird baths should be located in the garden and it should be cleaned every day. The water should be changed on a daily basis and the bottom should be rough and shallow so the birds will feel secure. It would be better if the bird bath can be viewed from a window so it is easier to observe the birds without distracting them.

When you finally get the hang of it, you might already have at least 25 bird species listed on your notepad or crossed out from your checklist. Casual bird watchers have different lists depending on the region that they often go birding in. By then, it is about time to visit other places. The best way to see more birds is to go to their natural habitat and watch them. Just like humans, birds have their own niche in nature. You can go to the nearest eco-park in your locality to widen your search and when your checklist records at least 100 species, it is about time to go to other states like Texas, Florida, Arizona, the Coast or Rio Grande, California and Colorado. The forests and the ocean are the best places to watch birds. It is expected that after visiting these states, your checklist will number at least 400 species. Of course, getting to that number will take dedication, passion and budget.

As your number of species accumulate, so will your enthusiasm and interest. This is the reason why it was said that bird watching is an addictive hobby. When you're already so deep in it, I'm sure you'd be planning to go to Australia, South Africa, Asia, Kenya, Costa Rica, the Amazon jungle, and Trinidad and Tobago.

Bird watching is indeed a worthwhile hobby. It is addicting, educational, interesting and, of course, it's fun.

Nature has a lot to offer us and bird-watching is an excellent method for us to realize how marvelous and diverse our surroundings actually are.

Chapter 2: Other Information of Birdwatching

It was only during the 18th century that people began to look at birds for aesthetics and observation purposes instead of food. The study of birds and their natural histories have then become prevalent in the Victorian Era, often associated with collection of eggs and stuffed birds on display. But later on, the awareness of the endangered numbers of certain species stopped the practice and "bird watching" became popular.

After that, guides to bird watching have sold hundreds of thousands of copies worldwide, with its audience ranging from bird lovers, to universities, and casual hobbyists.

Before the recent update in the list of endangered species, many birdwatchers only participate in observation activities. Now, with increasing public education on the welfare of these animals, birders now organize and participate in small and large-scale activities that aims to protect and conserve the remaining bird species populations and most preferably in their natural habitats. That is after citing of the dangers of captivity and enclosure. Bird watchers know that the birds are able to live the most when they are in the wild, instead of being kept in cages for "protection" purposes.

Other than these goodwill activities, birders also participate in sporting events relevant to their hobby. Birding events that are competitive in nature include the Big Day, Big Year and the Big Sit/Stay, that makes birders race on the numbers of species spotted and correctly identified within an area and time limit.

Nowadays, the networking and organizations of Birders allow the local birding communities to gather and share information with each other. Some bird species are even rescued from possible extinction with the joint efforts of these Non-Government Organizations.

Equipment in the hobby are constantly receiving upgrades just as fast as technological advances allow them to. Sighting, recording and identification equipment are under development to make the task easier, faster and more accurate.

Because of the increasing popularity of the hobby, the growing number of birders has become a concern for authorities. Regulations concerning bird watching etiquette have been put into place to make sure that the birds are not affected by their seasonal audience. And that the presence of these numbers of humans in their habitat will not affect the birds. These rules also cover the ethics and behavior a birder should take when relating to the other members of the community.

Within the birding community, the concern of these rules that have been placed, are particular in regards to stringing or the intentional recording of wrong or dubious ticks.

Popular bird watching shows have also contributed to the rise in the number of interested casual watchers as well as the dedicated birders in this community. Support has been increasing regarding programs that aim to preserve not only the birds, but also to protect their sanctuaries from "human invasion". There are actually universities that offer seasonal courses in birdwatching to allow students to both enjoy the activity and learn more about the ecology of the environment from one of the most visible representative of wildlife, the birds.

Chapter 3: Tools and Equipment

Ordinary bird-watching only requires you eyes, attention and your ears. But where is the fun in that? It will be more interesting if you have some basic equipment or tools you can use for a better and more convenient experience in bird-watching. Here are some of the basic tools you need.

1. Binoculars: A pair of binoculars is not mandatory but it is certainly useful especially since you cannot observe all birds up close. Plus, binoculars make it easier to observe birds you are able to spot on trees and they can be magnified for better identification. You don't need to buy expensive binoculars. But you want to make sure that it is lightweight, portable, and you'd be able to get a big, bright and crisp picture of a bird through it. Today, it is possible to buy an excellent pair of binoculars for a reasonable price. It can come with waterproof housing, accessories, and lifetime warranties as well. 7-power or 8-power binoculars are perfect for bird-watching. They offer excellent magnification and a wide angle so you can keep track of your bird while it hops from branch to branch. However, before that, you'd have to train your eyes to spot the birds, other animals and all movements in the scenery. It will be difficult to try to spot a bird on the binoculars alone. Pointing it in an already prospective spot is the key to use of binoculars and that means practice in scanning your view for the birds.

2. Notebook/Notepad: A pocket notebook is a necessity in bird-watching. You need to record a lot of information when you go out scouring for bird species. The notebook comes in handy when you cannot identify certain species. Take note of their accurate description as you see them and describe what you saw and heard. If you can sketch, it is definitely better. Just don't forget to use a pencil because ink can easily smudge when it rains on you and weather can sometimes be unpredictable. The size of the notebook depends on your usual set up. If you have a bag with you when birding, then those up to a medium size will do. However, if you're a portable birder who's more active and travel extra light, a notebook you can slip into your pocket will do. Decide the format of your notes beforehand so you won't be confused on what to write first when making your notes. Most people include "head", "beak/bill", "wings", "tail", "markings" and "behavior" in different but consistent arrangements in their notes.

3. Bird Book: Another term commonly used for bird book is field guide. It refers to a book on birds with illustrations and details about each species of bird. Although it is not mandatory, it is certainly helpful in identifying bird species. Avoid books that contain photographs as the colors tend to vary in different angles of light and camera lens and settings used by the photographer. Paintings and other drawn illustrations are better. Field guides are generally cheap and they are portable so it is better to bring one along. You never know when you will need it in the field so it's best to have it with you at all times. Of course, you need to note the region you will be birding in, as there are different sets of species that are frequently sighted in different regions.

4. Bird Feeders: Birds can be very aloof and when they are, it is difficult to observe them from afar. The best way to properly observe them is by letting them come to you. And how can you possibly do that? Well, feed them. Bird feeders lure the birds closer to you. Start with a black oil sunflower feeder, then hummingbird feeder in summer or try a suet feeder in winter. Whatever the season is, birds will come flocking to you when you have something readied for them. However, do remember bird watching etiquette and do not try to tame or approach them. After all the hobby is to watch them and not to collect or to pet.

5. Camera: Notes cannot always capture everything. It is not easy to observe birds as they are easily distracted. They can fly away even before you write a whole sentence. During these times, a camera will always do the trick. You can easily capture birds on film and study or identify them later. Recently, videos are becoming more popular too. With the advent of lightweight pocket video cameras, capturing videos of birds in flight and moving on the ground or from tree to tree have become much easier. Most of these cameras also have still capture functions that allows the user to take high-resolution photos. And because they can also sound, you can review your video clips for bird song identification.

6. Spotting Scope: Just like binoculars, a spotting scope can be very convenient especially when you have to observe certain species located quite far away from where you are standing. Birds aren't always found in one place. They are everywhere. You can spot them now and next thing you know, they are gone. Here comes the spotting scope. You can use it to spot birds perched on trees a quarter mile away. Plus you can also use you camera to capture bright and big images through your spotting scope. This technology is known as digiscoping.

7. Connections: If you are more comfortable going alone, then you probably don't need connections, but it is important to note that bird watching is a social activity that can be enjoyed by a lot of people together. It is more fun and exciting if it's done in groups because then you can share what you saw and heard with each other. Some can take notes, some can record and others can capture images. Bird-watching is also about connections in this way. Plus, there is the fact that you really learn a lot from other people you interact with. Most importantly, being an active part of the birding community will allow you to keep being updated with the latest news on the events and highlights of birding seasons.

8. Skills: You need some skills in order to be a good birder. You need to have keen eyes and ample attention to detail. These skills are needed in identifying bird species. You need some basic knowledge on what to observe and look for in birds. Remember to capture the color patterns, the size and shape, their behavior and the location and qualities of their habitat. You can learn bird watching skills if you are patient enough. You may find it difficult at first, since most people are used to ignoring small details like the birds on trees as they pass by them. However, it will get easier and even fun as you move along. Start noticing more, be patient, read more on the practice and apply it for experience.

9. Smart applications: If you have a smart phone, smart applications can be helpful in bird watching. Apps allow you to carry an entire bookshelf in your pocket. Some applications feature sounds and pictures of birds that can be very essential in bird identification. There are also applications that allow smart phone cameras to be paired with your binocular to take a photo of the spotted bird. There are also those that have bird song recorders and bird song libraries. These are helpful in identification and recordings.

10. Bird journal: This is like your diary on bird-watching. You can record everything from places you have been to every bird species you saw. In your journal, you can definitely document all the bird species you have observed and you can share it online with people who share the same passion and interest. It is different from your notebook because on that one, you'll only be making quick notes and mostly short-hand observations. In your journal, it can help to recall and record the entire experience and all details as accurately as possible, for each sighting associated with a certain bird. Journals can be written and recorded, either by date, with details of the number, species and other details of each bird watching trip, or by species or sighting, with details like time, date, experience, location and such. Decide on a format and style that gives you both the most details and that which suits you to write. Having a bird journal is great for comparison with other birders' experiences with the same species or season and insight for further observations can be made with them.

Other equipment used for bird watching is usually those that will either amplify or enhance the uses offered by the more basic tools in the activity. Many of them can be expensive and only the most dedicated birders collect and use them. For beginners, casual bird watchers, or those that wanted to do things old-school, the ten tools listed in this chapter is already enough to make the most of the bird watching experience.

Chapter 4: Bird-watching and Birding Terminologies

So, are you a bird-watcher or a birder? Is there even a difference between the two? What does the terms that you have read in the previous chapter meant? There are certain things and terms that you needed to know and should be aware of when beginning in the wonderful world of bird watching.

One of these is the seemingly unending debate on the right term for the hobbyist.

Some birders are offended when they are called bird-watchers. They are the serious ones who dedicate a large amount of time and resources to this hobby. Most casual bird-watchers would not know the difference between the two terms and are more likely to interchange them in use. That is perfectly alright when you're just in the hobby for the fun of it. But if you intend to be a serious, near-sporting birder, then you have to be careful and more informed when using birding terms. So, what is the difference between the two?

Although there are many people of types that enjoy both studying and watching birds, the two most common in the leisure and hobby area are the birders and bird-watchers. Realistically, those two terms are indeed interchangeable, but community customs have strong opinions on the matter. They both refer to individuals who studies and observes birds in their natural habitat. It will not matter what method they use, how experienced they are and how much passion they are exhibiting for the activity. It is the popular opinion among dedicated bird lovers that have made the difference between the two terms.

The term bird watching was first recorded in 1901, and thus older than the other. The term "bird" was not used as a verb before 1918 though. When the two terms became common use, there rose the debate on which is the term appropriate for the different kinds of people that observes birds as an enjoyment. Birding is often associated and used by those who treat the hobby with passion and often allocates more intensity in resources, time and attention to the activity. Bird watching was then more associated with casual bird observers and were not as involved with the birds. But, of course, birding is a term that is inclusive to the entire set of activities that are done when observing birds. After all, one does not only watch, but also listen and study the birds.

Along that line, we can say that bird watching is more casual, actually more focused on enjoying the birds and their natural habitat more than collecting species for their lists. These people enjoy the birds no matter where they are and do not mind if their list has too small a number of spotted species. They bird-watch wherever they go and are less likely to plan trips for that express reason. They appreciate the hobby through the years, possibly without intent to improve their field skills as painstakingly as birders. They can be as casual as just enjoying the visiting birds from the comfort of their home's window, as the birds are attracted by seasonally appropriate bird feeders placed in their backyards.

Just like the difference between a reader and a book collector, there are also the birders. They are also bird watchers, but they have set certain goals for themselves, and these are usually the lists of bird species that they wish to spot and observe within their lifetime. They are usually those that spend more money and are often avid about seeking new birds to watch. They would even travel long distances, just to sight seasonal migrations in an area and they have their own archives and records of their experiences. They are the most active ones in the birding community and are the ones who provide the best information for the more casual bird watchers about the best locations and the birds that can be found in those. They build up their knowledge about birds on their own and take measures to attract certain species into their area or backyards during the right seasons. They are also the ones who are best at educating people about the proper etiquette when observing and regarding birds in their natural habitat. Bird watching festivals usually have rules on these in place, so always check those out.

So, how can you tell if you're more of a bird watcher or a birder? This can be important when making your personal introductions and correspondences in a birding community. You can be whichever you prefer, no matter how you practice the hobby itself, but some of the guidelines that most communities observe include these:

- Bird-watchers usually own one or two field guides (a regional one and the other a more general scoped one) that they won't replace unless it's become unreadable, while birders would own updated editions of the most common regions that they'd frequent.
- Bird-watchers don't spend as much in upgrading their equipment while birders make it a point to have the best to make their observations more convenient and accurate. These include the best binoculars and other optics, as well as having multiple scopes aside from the regular equipment list for a bird-watcher.
- Bird-watchers have a life list or a yard list that they keep, but they don't usually markup many records. Birders, on the other hand, would have a yard list, a massive life list, year, trip, and season lists that they

usually keep in carefully organized archives for better navigation and indexing.

- Bird-watchers would go birding wherever they are, enjoying the birds, just as much as the scenery of their habitats, while birders would often go long distances just to spot a certain bird or to tick off their lists. They're often participants of bird festivals and would often arrange tours just to go birding.

- Bird-watchers try to identify the birds, but they don't make a big deal out of their mistakes, they would enjoy the birds either way. Birders would try their mightiest to accurately identify the birds, since they have quite large lists to fulfil. They would sometimes get disappointed to miss a bird other nearby birders have identified and would make multiple attempts to spot a certain species.

A person can be both a bird-watcher and a birder. Bird lovers often change their birding style to go with the season, day or the availability of their free time and the resources. Others may chase their new lifers or work hard to identify a rare visitor, but both of them have a love and respect of birds that fact will always be something that is beyond all the naming conflicts.

So we can move on from that, then.

Other than preparing your equipment, you will also have to study up on the nearly jargon-like words that you will hear around the birding community. In this chapter you will learn the basic and most common words and phrases used in the activity, as well as their definitions.

You can make use of a birding glossary, during your bird-watching, which are often available in contents of updated editions of field guides. These here are more casual terms that mean differently than those that you'll find in dictionaries, so you had better watch out. These are community-used terms that may also be different in other regions, but for your purpose, these are enough to append the formal terms found in the field guides. That said, tips on bird classification and others like that will be in another chapter to be discussed later and also for the most common birds found in the region.

Ornithologist: These are the actual scientists who study birds as their professions. They are usually called for certain requests like educational meetings, regional studies and species verification.

Birder: Birders are bird watchers who are keener than casual hobbyists, but not as obsessive as a twitcher. Birders are well-versed on the necessary knowledge in birding, from identification, to location, and environment. They usually assist newbie watchers with identifying their spotted birds and are indispensable to twitchers in finding the rare ones.

Stringer: Practically the worst insult you can hurl at a birder. This word refers to a person who always makes wrong identifications and still adds them to their life list. Those who find rarities, with little evidence to back them up, are often labeled as stringers. And the sightings of good ticks reported by those branded to be stringers are often treated by other birders with skepticism.

Twitcher: These birders are obsessive when it comes to their lists. They would often go after rare birds sighted by their friends and the others within their community. They may even go on an impromptu trip halfway across the country just to watch a drab, but rare bird from half a kilometer away. Their lists are overly large and usually impress only other twitchers. Despite these, they are mostly not that good with identification and usually rely on their fellow birders' skills to correctly ID spotted birds for them. Although this may seem negative, the term to "twitch" is also a verb that meant to go somewhere to find or observe a rarity. This is an activity that you don't necessarily have to be a twitcher to do. Different kinds of birders do convene to twitch a rare sighting.

Blocker: When a very rare bird appears on the regional list, but you weren't able to see it when others luckily did, then you are "blocked" and this bird is your blocker, because you probably never will have the chance to try again.

Bogey Bird: A bogey bird is that certain bird that you have missed a number of times, despite having your companions spotting it many times.

BOP: Bird of Prey, you know them, they're awesome and easy to spot due to their size and hunting behavior.

To dip (or a dipper): It means to miss a bird that you were waiting to spot in an area. Experienced birders often say that the farther you go for a single bird, the bigger the chance it is to dip that bird. A bird that you have missed is called a dipper. Dipping a single species a number of times make it your bogey bird.

First: It is the first record of a bird species in a specific area, or a defined region, for example, an Australian first.

IBA: Important Birding Area. These birding spots are considered to be important in the conservation and protection of the birds in the area. Oftentimes, more stringent rules in birding practice are applied here.

Jizz (or Gizz): It is the overall impression that can be identified with the combination of the general shape, behavior, movement and other easy to spot attribute of a species, rather than spotting specific features. With enough experience, birders can use the jizz to ID their birds and can be done with even a distanced or fleeting sights. If you have become able to identify the more common species with bare eyesight, then you had used the jizz to do so. This commonly used term came from the WW2 slang for the identification of planes by their General Impression, Shape and Size (GISS).

LBJ: "Little Brown Job"; Many birds are brown, small and plain-looking. They look mostly alike and make species identification quite tricky. Immature and female birds are the most probable LBJs and even experts get difficulties in making accurate IDs on them.

Lifer: Is a birder's first sighting of a species. They are called as such because you get to add it to your life list, therefore, a "lifer".

List: It is the list of all the species observed by a single observer. Most birders have a life list for their regional birds and another one for the world list, if they have the means to travel abroad. They could also have a yard list or a provincial one that is smaller and have species with near regular sightings. Some hobbyists compete for the number of species in their lists and the ones with the highest numbers are the "listers". Many local birding groups also have acknowledgements to their communities own listers.

Mega: Term used to refer to a very rare species. Birders would usually congregate upon the news of the arrival or spotting of one. If you're not quick enough, you might end up with an expensive and disappointing dipper.

Megatick: A Megatick is a tick on your list that is extremely good. The factors are usually species rarity and its difficulty to find, identify and observe. A megatick would only be considered as such when there are other birders, and even veterans that would also consider it a good tick.

Newmans, Sasol, Sinclairs, and Roberts: These are the common names that refer to the four most popular field guides used in birding. You'll have to choose which one suits your region best. Editions are updated every few years, but even older ones are quite reliable, as the new ones are often just updated with new species and the new migration patterns as well as the changes in common behaviors in the species.

String: A record or list that is doubtful. Usually treated as such by coming from a previously proven stringer (liar) and has rare ticks that are not backed by a substantial record and evidence.

Tick: marking a species off one of your lists or adding a species to that particular list.

There are many other terms used in the birding community that you will find in forums and other publications. With time, you will be able to familiarize yourself with their meanings and usage. Be careful though, just like any jargon, misusing them could make you look like a pretender, so always be sure of what you are saying.

Chapter 5: Bird-watching Tips for Beginners

As much as birds are interesting to look at, watching them can be quite challenging. Birds are energetic and playful in nature. Sometimes they are everywhere and sometimes they are nowhere. You need patience and keen eyesight to observe them better and you need to be as quick as possible as they tend to get distracted easily and fly away. They are also quick movers and tend to flick everywhere even in a single spot. There are also a lot of other obstacles like the sun, the bushes, the silhouette, or the darkness. So, for beginners, here are some important tips you can use to better identify the bird species and know what matters most in order to spend quality bird-watching time.

1. Focus on the bird: The bird is the primary and the most important subject in bird-watching so you must focus on the bird as soon as you spot it. Avoid flipping through the pages of your bird book right away. Observe it first. Look at the marking on its body, movements, behavior, flight patterns and eating habits. If you need to really take down notes, make it quick or do it while making sure that the bird is still on sight. Remember, every chance you have to watch the bird shouldn't be taken for granted. Bird-watching time is precious so make use of the time wisely and creatively. With practice, you will be able to burn the bird's details into your mind and jot down your notes when you're sure that you the bird had really flown away and you're not going to be able to observe it longer.

2. Be attentive and use your ears: Birds and humans have some things in common. That is, they both rely on their senses of hearing and sight to interact with others of their kind. The sounds of their chirps and calls are distinct in every species. Their songs can be used to identify their classification and family. There are some species of birds that are very difficult to identify unless you hear them sing. Just like the nightingales or the hummingbirds. They are not very easy to spot on but their voices can make it easier for the bird watchers to identify them. There are also other bird species that can look very similar and the only faster way to differentiate them is their voice just like the willow warblers and chiffchaffs. It's also easy to do it while watching the bird. In a place where many birds gather, it would be beneficial in identification if you match the beak/bill movements with the correct call/song in the sea of sounds. It's important to be able to associate the right song with the one that you're currently observing.

Here are the things you need to watch out for when listening to the birds:

- **Tempo**: Listen carefully and count the beats of each bird song. Is it quick or is it slow? Make sure that you look at the bill to check if it synchronizes with the sound that you hear.

- **Pitch**: You also have to take note of the pitch. Is it high or low? If it changes, at which part of the song does it change?

- **Volume**: Does the song or the voice become softer or louder?

- **Repetition**: Listen and focus on the repetition as well. Does the bird repeat a certain syllable in the song or not?

- **Length**: It refers to how long the songs go on.

With enough experience or even by listening to audio archives of bird songs, you will be able to identify species by song. There are of course similar songs across species and that is why sighting is still the primary identification you'd want to use. There are also convenient applications that can be downloaded to your different devices that can be used for recording, playback and archiving your audio library of bird calls and songs to be used for comparison.

3. Identify the bird carefully: The goal of bird-watching is not only to see birds but to be able to identify them as well. There are different ways to identify bird species easier and more efficiently. One way is to make use of spotting scopes and binoculars. The best bird watchers use the best kind of binoculars. The better your equipment is, the more effective you can be in spotting and identifying bird species. If you are using a cheap kind of binoculars or lenses, you wouldn't be able to see clearly when the bird is more than a hundred meters away from you. But if you are skilled enough with the use of one, then you will be able to identify birds accurately even with a cheap binoculars. Binoculars are best used to spot birds in motion or in flight. When spotting birds resting in foliage, a keen eye to spotting the most often motionless bird from its background is important. As mentioned before when identifying bird species, take note of their size, shape, bill characteristics, legs and feet, facial and body markings as well as their tail and colors. It is important to note that birds do not always look the same as they look in the books. Their color patterns change with season and those that are different between genders. There are also some birds which turn fluffier under certain situations. Study their flight patterns and eating habits. And of course, that includes being familiar with the species themselves.

What you need to take note of when identifying the bird:

- **General Size and Shape**: A general impression of the bird, including its shape and size can often help in the primary identification you can do on the spot. You'll easily be able to identify which family it belongs to by noting size and shape. Making references to the more common birds can be your measure for it.

- **Facial Markings and Bill**: These are the first things you should pay attention to the moment you lock on a bird. Many species have distinctive head features and include their eyes, face feathers and their bill. It would also be a huge clue to their habits.

- **Body, Tail Shape and Wing Bars**: After the head, focus on the body and observe the markings, patterns, patches and other distinctive feature that can help you identify the bird's species. Even the shape and how they hold their tail are attributes that differ across the species, so you better take note.

- **Leg Length and Color**: Whether it is short or long legged, if you can get a glimpse of the legs, it will be better for you, as they can easily identify the species with that. Also, notice the color and the way the toes formed or are arranged, if you can see them.

- **Flight and Movement**: How does it "walk"? How does it hold its tail? How does it move along the branches? How does it fly? Swooping or gliding, high up or straight down, details about a bird's movement can help pin-point its species.

- **Feeding Habits**: If you can watch the birds feeding its food and feeding pattern can tell a lot about a bird. You might even be able to differentiate between a local and a visitor as birds feed differently across regions, despite being in the same species. An example are the different feeding habits of a kingfisher or "bluebird" from different areas.

Since more often than not, all you will have to observe a bird is a few seconds; you have to learn to get as much detail with every spotting. It will require focus and memory, so it will not do to have distractions around and it is a skill set that need constant practice. If you're able to do it, you will be surprised at the number of species that you'd be able to see, not just among birds but also for other small animals that have often escaped your notice.

4. Observe their habitat, climate and region: Wherever you may be, you will normally see birds that are more popular in that region. So when you go for bird-watching, make sure that you are equipped with knowledge on their habitats, climate and regions. Do you see them near the lakes or in the seashores? Are they always perched on tree tops? Do they like staying on the ground or in the mudflats? Do you only see them during summer or winter? Their habitats, the climate and the region will tell you what to look for and expect in a specific area. If you know what to expect and where to look for the birds, bird-watching becomes easier and enjoyable and your time is not wasted.

5. Interact with other bird-watchers: Beginners need to really interact with other birders. There are so many things you still don't know and you can learn many things when you interact with your fellow birders. Others will definitely be willing to share their knowledge and sightings with you as well as some good photographs. That way, bird-watching becomes more enjoyable and learning becomes more exciting. Always respect people you meet during birding and you will get the same respect in return. The birding community is a friendly one and it could become quite the extended family for those who are open and cooperative.

6. Take notes: It is inevitable that there are some bird species which cannot be identified right away especially the endangered species or those that are migratory to the area. In this case, it is necessary to take down notes regarding the details of what you have observed on that particular bird. It is important to notice physical attributes and markings on the bird especially the bill characteristics, plumage, the voice and song, the tails and flight patterns and the color. Always record anything of note during your birding sessions. You can also practice your memory and note-taking by jotting down details of a fleeting bird sighting you've had, like when you're in a moving vehicle, or you've spotted one while biking and such. Make it a habit to have your notebook and pencil in close reach wherever you go, because you never know when you're going to encounter a lifer and birds are practically everywhere.

7. Have fun and Patience is the key: Bird-watching is certainly not for the impatient. Birds are naturally unpredictable and so it takes a lot of patience to be able to observe each species properly. There are times when you have to wait at night just so you can see them in their natural habitat especially the owls and other nocturnal birds, you may also go and observe other night creatures such as the bats. There are also those instances that you cannot identify the bird from afar. You would need to somehow make the birds come closer to you and so you have to feed them daily for them to feel secure around you. If you are not patient, it is better for you to look for a different hobby because certainly bird-watching is not for you.

You may have already gotten a few good tips on this chapter on the things that you need to pay attention to. Especially the details when observing the birds that you needed to remember and note afterwards. The next chapter will discuss these more in detail.

Chapter 6: Tips on How to Identify Bird Species

Knowledge of birds is not mandatory but it is helpful. You actually don't need to learn everything about birds to be able to watch them freely. They are naturally interesting and cute and charming in their own right. In bird watching, you'd naturally feel the urge to identify each species and you will definitely ask yourself "What bird is it?" The ultimate end goal of bird-watching is to be able to identify the kind of bird you are watching.

Bird identification in North America is an exciting endeavor. In the US and Canada alone, it will be very challenging to find at least 500 species out of the reported 970. Apart from optional equipment for your convenience, your eyes, ears, and mind are the most important things to be active while bird-watching. So, here are some of the most important points to remember when identifying bird species.

1. Color: Birds are colorful beings. Since they rely on visual and hearing to communicate, the color of their feathers and other physical characteristics are very important to note when you are trying to identify bird species. It is a must to note as much details on their color as you can. Look for the basic color on the upper parts as these colors indicate important clues as to what species they belong to. Upperparts include the wings and the back while the under parts refer to the tail, belly, and head.

Ensure that you capture which color is more prominent. Bright color patches are very easy to distinguish. For example, if you see a bright bluish patch on the wing it will more likely tell you that you are looking at a jay while a yellow wing and a red face will give you the goldfinch. Look for any visible physical and body markings. Do you see any stripes around or above the eyes? Are there any colorful streaks on the chest? Do you see bars on the wings? Are the feathers a little pale than most of the body colors or is it all the same? Is the tail the same color as the back of the bird?

Aside from looking at these things, one should always take into consideration that there are a lot of factors affecting the colors of the birds. First, the lighting and the viewing angle can affect the color of the plumage. Second, the age of the bird also affects the color as younger birds tend to have a different color from adults of their respective species. And third, plumage changes with season.

Make sure that you observe the bird both when it is in flight and stationary. The back and the belly should be observed. How long are the tail and the body? What does the tail look like? Is it rounded, forked, or square? Try to observe the color of the legs and the length as well, as mentioned in the previous chapter. Are they long or short? Are the feet webbed that indicates they live near water or do they have talons which indicate predatory behavior? If you can be lucky enough to watch them up close, count the toes that point backwards and those that point forwards. These are also clues to their habits and movement patterns, and some species have distinctive sets of those.

2. Shape: When you try to identify the bird species, you have to look at the shape as well. In here you need to take notice of the legs and feet as well as the bill or the bird's beak. Picture the bird as a whole. Silhouettes are the best method to determine the shape of the bird. Is it rounded or elongated? Is it a little close to being oblong?

Check on the head first, since it is one of the more distinct between species, and the more difficult part to observe. Is it rounded or does it appear to be hooded? Do the feathers form like a crest on top of its head? Aside from the strips and patches of colors on the head, look into the eye markings and shape as well. Look at the length and shape of the bill. Is it longer than the length of the body or shorter? What about the shape of the bill? Is it conical, flat, elongated, rounded, pointed, curved or straight? For example, if the bird has a stout and short bill, more likely it belongs to the seed eaters like the sparrow or the finch. Birds of prey on the other hand usually have hooked bill and are typically large in size.

3. Size: If the bird is in flight, it is difficult to determine the size so make sure to just compare it with other birds in flight as well. Poor lighting conditions also make it difficult to measure the bird size. Generally speaking, the best way to get the approximate size of the bird is to compare it with other familiar bird species. Does it appear to be small or big? Is it larger than the pigeon or smaller than a robin? Is it as large as an owl or bigger than a falcon? With enough experience, you will be able to make the proper estimates at different distances without the need for references to other species. That is also as well because a different species flying with the one you're observing might not always be present. It is also important to note their way of walking on land. Do they appear to be walking awkwardly or unsteady? Or do they walk with ease?

Does it appear larger in flight because of its wingspan? Don't forget to note the movements and flight patterns as well. Do they glide steadily and gently on air or do they flap their wings up and down in every wing beat? This difference is between gliding and swooping. Gliders are those that fly longer distances, fish or hunt in the air. Birds that swoop up and down when flapping their wings are usually seed, fruit or insect eaters that don't need to be as careful with the repercussions of their flight. Swooping patterns in flight also indicate shorter distances between rests. They are more likely to flutter from tree to tree than gliders who prefer to fly in more open spaces. When they walk, do they hold their tail up and how about when they jump from one tree branch to the other?

4. Habitat: Habitat is another important factor to consider when identifying bird species. Do they usually stay in mud flats or near the sea shore? Are they always perched on tree tops? Do they like the grasslands or the forests? Although some birds will be commonly found anywhere, there are still certain types of birds which prefer to stay in one place. These types are easily distinguishable through their habitat. Even migratory birds have preferred resting places, so if you know what species you are looking for, watch out for the spots that they may likely choose to land in.

5. Songs and calls: There are certain species of birds that are easier to identify by their sounds rather than their physical attributes. Voice of birds is generally helpful especially when they seem to be in hiding. Songs are usually created by male bird species to defend their territories and to attract mates. In some other species, however, like the blackbirds and cardinal, as well as wrens, females also use their voices to sing but it's generally weaker and softer than that of the males of their respective species. Calls are generally used between most species to communicate with each other. They call to warn of predators, to solicit for some food, to court the female species, and to deter unwanted intruders in their territories. If you are not familiar with bird songs and calls, it is definitely helpful if you can have a recording of their songs and calls and memorize it. That way you will easily notice and recognize the song or the sound when you hear it. There are useful bird song archives found in many sources, and there are now smart phone applications with birdsong from the most common species.

Bird identification is not as easy as flipping through your field guide. It has to be practiced all the time to increase efficiency and accuracy. If you want to identify the bird you spot when bird-watching, then you will have to get familiar with both the local and regional species. You may also want to include the seasonal ones in that, those that visit your locality during certain months of the year. After all, you never know when your next lifer will appear and it would be a waste to dip on it just because you cannot ID it correctly.

Chapter 7: 10 Most Popular Bird Species in America

There are hundreds of reported species residing in the region, but only a few that you could easily observe in your immediate surroundings. As a beginner, it is wise to start practicing bird identification with this list. Here are the 10 most popular bird species in the American continent. Included are the basics in their identification, but to practice the advice from the previous chapters, you have to learn the rest from experience. Do not be discouraged with a few mishaps with identification during your first tries. Everyone makes mistakes at first. And you might think that you look too much of a newbie when you often consult your field guide and other bird books. But remember, you're only beginning and you're yet to be familiar with the birds and the practices in this hobby, so it is alright to be as bookish as you need to be. It is better to make mistakes, try again and make accurate identifications than become a stringer just trying to appear knowledgeable on the first go.

Here is the list of Continental America's top 10 most commonly observed bird species that is the perfect starting off point in your birding career:

1. Mourning Dove: These are very common across the entire American continent. It has a slender tail, graceful movements and a small head. They are very fast in flight and they exhibit bullet straight flight patterns. These species are the most frequently hunted in North America. They are called mourning doves because their call sounds like a lament with its drawn-out and soft voice.

2. Northern Cardinal: Both the male and female northern cardinals are enchantingly beautiful. The males sport a red plumage with a crest on their head while females can be brownish or pink, sometimes seen as orange-like under different lightings. They are seen all year round because they don't migrate. Even in winter, their color remains bright adding to the pale and all white background of the snow. During summer, their beautiful song is the first you will hear in the morning. They are small and energetic, but they are territorial and more likely to be upfront when in their nesting tree. With this, they are easier to spot out among the greens.

3. Downy Woodpecker: This is probably one of the most popular species of woodpeckers in the American continent. They are distinguished through their black and white plumage and they have a nub of a bill. Male downy woodpeckers have a red spot on their nape while females don't. They are usual backyard guests and they feed on suet, nuts, seeds, and fruits. They are easy to recognize and so most bird-watchers are able to master these species among others. Another attribute to note is their popular, distinctive calls and sounds.

4. Dark-eyed Junco: These are winter inhabitants of Northern America. Before winter they are seen in Canada and the Western mountains. They are quite easy to recognize with their varied and crisp markings as well as the bright and white tail feathers which they show off habitually when they are in flight. They belong to the sparrow family.

5. Blue Jay: Blue jays are large songbirds distinguished for their plumage tinged with bright blue, black and white, noisy calls and perky crest. They are believed to be intelligent and their family bonds are tight. They are the saviors of the oak trees during the late glacial period thanks to their love for acorns. You can actually attract visiting jays to your backyard with a well-chosen feeder. You may even have some roost in your backyard during certain months of their activity.

6. American Goldfinch: American goldfinch males sport a bright yellow with a bit of black and white tinge during summer while females and other winter birds have duller colors. Their tails are notched and pointed and their bills are conical. Their feathers molt in the winter and they look bizarrely patchy. They also have wing bars. The American goldfinch is the state bird of Washington, Iowa and New Jersey.

7. Black-capped Chickadee: These species are very curious about anything including humans. They have a very small body and an oversized round head which never fails to attract everyone's attention. This universally "cute" chickadee is distinct with its white cheeks, black bib and cap, grayish tails, wings and back, puffy sides and whitish underside. They are always around people and feeders, investigating everything in their territory.

8. American crow: American crows are highly intelligent and they are large with cawing and hoarse voices. They are found anywhere in the entire American continent and they are black all over. They can live anywhere from treetops, city center, beaches, roadsides, open woods and fields. They eat on the ground feeding on earthworms, fruits, seeds, smaller animals, insects and even garbage, chicks and carrion. Their flight pattern is distinct and it is rarely disrupted with graceful glides. It is a methodical, patient, and unique way of flapping. They are social birds, so expect to see more when you spot one, although a lone flier is not that rare.

9. Tufted Titmouse: The tufted titmouse has large black eyes, a brushy crest and a small but rounded bill. They live in deciduous forests and they are often seen where feeders abound. These birds are gray and small and they have echoing sounds. They are playful and when they find a large seed they will happily carry it with them and whack it with their stout bill.

10. House Finch: They are new in the American neighborhood but they received a warmer welcome than other arrivals like the House sparrow and European Starling. The house finch has a red breast and head for males and their song is a long twit. Today, they are found everywhere in North America as well as in Hawaii. You can easily attract them into your property with easy to make feeders and adequate sized nesting houses up in a tree or a pole shielded from stiffer winds.

There are many that might be most common than these 10 when it comes to North America, but because these are the most popular among the common but significant species, you can make it your initial goal list.

Chapter 8: Top 20 Birding Locations in North America

As already mentioned, birds are practically everywhere in continental America. You only need to know where and how to look. The country has hundreds of species frequenting their favorite spots all over the region. As a new birder, you can start off with your own back yard off course, adding your neighborhood and nearby places to gain more experience. Once you have gained enthusiasm and experience in birding and you've already ticked off most of your local list, then you could check out these birding locations in North America that yielded birders with quite the finds for their life lists.

1. **Big Bend, Texas [11th]:** The Big Bend national Park that extends along the Mexican border from the Rio Grande has the highest number of recorded bird species in the United States. There are reported to be nearly 450 species that can be sighted in this park. So if you are ready for more and unique bird-watching experience, you can take a hike or even drive around the park. Some of the local specialty birds that are sought after in this area are the Zone-tailed hawks, the Colima Warblers, Gray-breasted Jays, the Scaled Quail, Chihuahuan Raven s and the Lucifer Hummingbirds.

2. **Bosque del Apache, New Mexico [18th]:** This classic western landscape boasts of the loud calls of the Snow Geese as well as the Ross' Geese that flock in the area. There are also the trumpeting Sandhill Cranes. Other common birds in the area are the Northern Pintails, Mallards, and the Green-winged Teal. Most active during the autumn and winter

seasons, you would want to visit the Bosque del Apache national park for these magnificent birds.

3. **Cape May, New Jersey [2nd]:** This series of marshes and coastal woods in the southern tip of New Jersey have been home to some of the best spring and fall bird species. Waves upon waves of songbirds, shorebirds, waterfowl and raptors, as well as migrating seabirds, flock into the coasts. Even single species count can reach thousands on good sighting. With more than 400 species reported to be seasonally spotted in the area, it is definitely one of the best spots to visit.

4. **Churchill, Manitoba [7th]:** This is the most popular of all the birding spots in Canada. Since it is where the tundra forest and the boreal one merge here near Churchill River and Hudson Bay, this area offers the diversity of species that each had. Common Eiders, Pacific Loons, Tundra Swans, Oldsquaws, Stilt sandpipers, Golden Plovers, Hudsonian Godwits, Longspurs, and a variety of ducks can be found in this area. There are harder to find species like the Northern Shrikes, Bohemian Waxwings and Gray-cheeked Thrushes.

5. **Dry Tortugas, Florida [19th]:** This area, best to visit from mid-April through the first ten days of May, is the fallout area for migrating songbirds during a weather system pushover. There are many warbler species that gather there in such instances and others like the Orchard Orioles, Tanagers, Buntings and Black-billed Cuckoos are also spotted there. Seabirds can also be spotted if you join one of the boat tours that can bring you near the nesting

spots to these birds that include Tropicbirds, Frigatebirds, gannets and Terns.

6. **Hakalau Forst, Hawaii [17th]:** The protected forest with a wide range of foliage allowed the development of a vast range of bird species in the area. They include the most spectacular birds in the world and definitely a goal to every birder's life list.

7. **Kalamath Basin [10th]:** Just below the Mount Shasta, geese, ducks and other raptors that include the Bald Eagle can be sighted in these areas. The large number of geese and ducks flocking in the area attracts a large variety of predatory birds like the eagle, Hawks, Harriers and red-tails.

8. **Kidder County, North Dakota [8th]:** This least known amazing birding spot offers sights of many nesting ducks, raptors, shorebirds and some amazing grassland songbirds. Pelicans and hawks are also seen at the Chase Lake National Wildlife Refuge. But some of the common finds include the burrowing Owls and different species of sparrows in the areas where the crops have been cut short.

9. **Lower Rio Grande Valley, Texas [6th]:** This area has birds that you could call Mexican immigrants. They have hopped across the border and are rarely seen anywhere farther north. Do not miss the chance to see the offers of prime birding spots like the Santa Ana and Lower Rio Grande National Wildlife Refuge, Falcon State Park, Bentsen State Park, Laguna Atascosa national Wildlife Refuge, and the Sabal Palm Grove Sanctuary.

10. **Machias Seal Island [20th]:** This? Just a few words: Atlantic Puffins, Razorbills, Arctic and

Common terns, Common Murres, Leach Storm Petrels and the Great Cormorants. You might also be interested in Bald Eagles, Common Loons, Ospreys and have I mentioned Puffins?

11. **Monterey Bay, California [13th]:** This area is a definite stop in sea birds passing this side of the Pacific Coast. These included the large-spanned Albatrosses and many other fall and winter cruisers. Rarer birds can be sighted by taking a trip to the Seavalley fifteen to twenty-five miles offshore.

12. **Nome, Alaska [16th]:** Previously settled as a gold-mining town, this is certainly the gold mine for bird-watchers. It is the best birding spot to sight Arctic species and the much-sought Grylfalcon. There are many shorebirds that can be seen even offseason and their breeding displays are definitely sights to be seen.

13. **Platte River, Nebraska [12th]:** Sandhill Cranes and Grouse dance around the areas in the remnant prairies of the area each March. You can also search for Bald Eagles and Snow Geese.

14. **Point Pelee Ontario [5th]:** The most popular of the Canadian birding locations, this is a passage for many migration birds. With many passing songbirds, waterbirds, shorebirds, gulls, waterfowl, raptors, terns and gulls, you will see wonderful species like Tundra Swans and about 42 species of warblers.

15. **Pribilof Islands, Alaska [9th]:** The cliffs in these islands attract colonies of thousands of seabirds as well as birders for the birds of the Bering Sea. Red-faced cormorants, Auklets and parakeets

are only some of those that can be seen here. With trails dedicated to birdwatchers, this is a great place to watch for the cold North Pacific Ocean species.

16. **Sand Lake, South Dakota [15th]:** Fall migration brings some of the most colorful bird species into this area. From pelicans to grebes, coots and ducks, as well as half a million mallards and gulls amass in this region during their migration. Although waterfowl are the main attractions in the area, there are also a variety of grassland species that will surely catch your sights, like the ring-necked Pheasant.

17. **Snake River Valley, Idaho [14th]:** This is the place where you can spot the largest concentration of nesting birds of prey. Raptor watchers travel here to the Snake River BOP natural Area where you can spot hawks, falcons, harriers and the Golden Eagles.

18. **Southeast Arizona [3rd]:** One of the best birding spots in the Old West Region, the old cowboy towns of Tucson and Tombstone are great stops for going to the Chihuahuas, Huachucas and the Santa Ritas for birds that can be encountered south of the border with Mexico.

19. **South Florida [1st]:** Unrivaled among birding hotspots in the region, it is one of the best choices in all of North America, going through the species that can be found here is like the true Birding Odyssey from the ding Darling National Wildlife Refuge to the Corkscrew Swamp and finally to the Everglades. From roseate Spoonbills, storks and many other large bird species, you'll surely enjoy the variety here.

20. Upper Texas Coast [4th]: When you say birding complexes, this spot is one of the best. Wintering birds like the endangered Whooping Cranes can be found here. They are really rare and few, now numbering at just 155. Boat trips get you to see them and other wading birds like the egrets and waterfowls.

There are many other spots in continental America that would have made it to the top in terms of the species offered, but these are the most common and popular choices among experienced birders that often visit annually during these areas' seasonal peaks.

After you've taken your fill (and ticked off your list) of the species that frequent the continent, you can then plan on to see those species that are endemic to certain countries. You can even do it off-hand. You don't have to be so keen on finding these. Just bring your equipment every time you travel and you'll be ticking off your list while you relax, in no time.

Join a local birding group in your community or share and get info with those from other regions via the Internet. Just remember the Birder's etiquette and be honest all the time! The birding community is respectful and friendly, but they are also quite passionate and would not excuse intentional stringing, remember that!

After this "beginner's manual" you can start devouring more birding books that will tackle the grittier parts of the activity. The devil is in the details so they say. Have your very first field guide to supplement this book and then you're good to go. Do not be shy to ask for help, since you're just learning. Bird watching is one of the best ways to fill your days with sights of nature and of education towards a better understanding and awareness of your place in this Earth.

You might even discover a way to save not just the birds, buts some other endangered species too!

Now that you know how, where, what to look for, and what you need to be able to start you adventures bird watching, all you need to do now is look out your window and spot your first bird! Make every day count and make bird watching a daily activity for you and your friends. Not only will this help hone your bird watching skills, this will also shape your senses to become sharper, a trait that will definitely benefit you beyond the requirements of birdwatching.

Conclusion

Thank you again for purchasing this book!

I hope this book was able to help you to better recognize and identify bird species in continental America.

The next step is to go out there and start bird-watching. Start in your own backyard. Follow the tips and reminders I gave you and observe American bird species in their natural habitat. You will realize in no time that bird-watching is much more enjoyable and worthwhile than other hobbies you can possibly think of.

Finally, if you enjoyed this book, please take the time to share your thoughts and post a review on Amazon. We do our best to reach out to readers and provide the best value we can. Your positive review will help us achieve that. It'd be greatly appreciated!

Thank you and good luck!